Zdravstvujtye, RUSSIA

by Meghan Gottschall

CHERRY LAKE PUBLISHING • ANN ARBOR, MICHIGAN

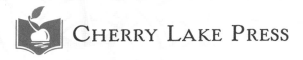

CHERRY LAKE PRESS

Published in the United States of America by Cherry Lake Publishing Group
Ann Arbor, Michigan
www.cherrylakepublishing.com

Reading Advisor: Marla Conn, MS, Ed., Literacy specialist, Read-Ability, Inc.

Photo Credits: ©DigitalVision Vectors/jack0m/Getty Images, cover (globe): ©iStock/SchulteProductions/Getty Images, cover (top): ©E+/Raatzie/Getty Images, cover (bottom): ©E+/Mordolff/Getty Images, 1: ©E+/07_av/Getty Images, 3: ©Moment/Mr. Anujak Jaimook/Getty Images, 4: ©Moment/Sergey Pesterev/Getty Images, 5: ©iStockphoto/Getty Images, 6: ©iStockphoto/Getty Images, 7 (bottom): ©E+/avdeev007/Getty Images, 7 (top): ©iStockphoto/Getty Images, 8: ©Moment/Kitti Boonnitrod/Getty Images, 9: ©iStockphoto/Getty Images, 10: ©Westend61/Getty Images, 11: ©iStockphoto/Getty Images, 12 (bottom): ©iStockphoto/Getty Images, 12 (top): ©iStockphoto/Getty Images, 13: ©iStockphoto/Getty Images, 14 (bottom): ©Beinecke Library/Wikimedia, 14 (top): ©Westend61/Getty Images, 15: ©Moment/Anton Petrus/Getty Images, 16: ©Moment/Matt Anderson Photography/Getty Images, 18 (top): ©E+/Mlenny/Getty Images, 18 (bottom): ©iStock Editorial/Elen11/Getty Images, 19: ©Burak Kara/Getty Images, 20: ©iStockphoto/Getty Images, 21: ©iStock Editorial/Vadim_Orlov/Getty Images, 22: ©Photodisc/David De Lossy/Getty Images, 23: ©carolround/Pixabay, 24 (bottom): ©INeverCry/Wikimedia, 24 (top): ©Kekyalyaynen/Shutterstock, 25: ©Moment/Sharon Vos-Arnold/Getty Images, 26: ©iStockphoto/Getty Images, 27: ©E+/brusinski/Getty Images, 28: ©iStock Editorial/ermess/Getty Images, 30: ©Sarycheva Olesia/Shutterstock, 31: ©marsjo/Pixabay, 32: ©EyeEm/Getty Images, 33: ©Editorial RF/zorazhuang/Getty Images, 34: ©iStockphoto/Getty Images, 35: ©Moment/Wendy Rauw Photography/Getty Images, 37: ©iStockphoto/Getty Images, 38: ©Moment/Verdina Anna/Getty Images, 39 (top): ©Moment/Ekaterina Smirnova/Getty Images, 39 (bottom): ©Iuliia Kochenkova/Shutterstock, 40: ©iStockphoto/Getty Images, 41 (bottom): ©Moment/Boris SV/Getty Images, 41 (top): ©Larisa Rudenko/Shutterstock, 42: ©iStockphoto/Getty Images, 43: ©iStockphoto/Getty Images, 44: ©Iakov Filimonov/Shutterstock, 45: ©DigitalVision Vectors/filo/Getty Images, background

Cherry Lake Press is an imprint of Cherry Lake Publishing Group.

Library of Congress Cataloging-in-Publication Data has been filed and is available at catalog.loc.gov

Cherry Lake Publishing Group would like to acknowledge the work of the Partnership for 21st Century Learning, a Network of Battelle for Kids. Please visit http://www.battelleforkids.org/networks/p21 for more information.

Printed in the United States of America
Corporate Graphics

TABLE OF CONTENTS

CHAPTER 1

WELCOME TO RUSSIA!

Moscow International Business Center is a brand-new district of the city and includes many of Europe's tallest buildings.

Russia is a vast country with snowy plains in the east and busy cities in the west. It is the largest nation in the world, spanning two continents. The country stretches 5,600 miles (9,000 kilometers) across northern Europe and Asia. It takes up about one-ninth of the land on Earth.

Russia has many neighbors. Fourteen countries share its border. The longest borders are with Kazakhstan, China, and Mongolia. There are also three ocean borders: the Atlantic, Arctic, and Pacific.

The country's long history has created a rich culture. It is known for classical music and ballet. Religious art and architecture fill cities and towns. Many people read and study great works of Russian literature. Let's explore this diverse country!

Siberia is one of the most sparsely populated areas on Earth.

ACTIVITY

Take a close look at the map of Russia. Trace the outline of the country on a separate piece of paper. Draw a star to mark where Moscow is. Find an atlas or locate a map of Russia online. Label the bordering countries. How many did you find? Which countries are in Asia? Which ones are in Europe?

The Ural Mountains mark the divide between Europe and Asia within Russia. Around 75 percent of the land is on the Asian side.

The region of Siberia is east of the Urals. It makes up most of the central and eastern parts of the country. Northern Siberia is known for its **tundra**. Only certain plants and grasses grow in the frosty soil.

The Angara River drains Siberia's Lake Baikal.

White Nights

Some parts of Russia are so far north that they experience "white nights." This happens just south of the Arctic Circle. From mid-May to mid-July, the sun barely sets. For a few hours every night, the sky appears white. The sun rises around 3:00 a.m. St. Petersburg hosts the White Nights Festival. There are performances, fireworks, and a pretend pirate battle on a river.

South of the tundra is the taiga. This is a zone of coniferous, or evergreen, forests. The taiga stretches from the Urals to the Pacific Ocean. Treeless plains called steppes are south of the taiga. These grasslands are good for farming.

The steppes stretch across much of Russia.

Mount Elbrus has two peaks, both of which are dormant volcanic domes.

Mountain ranges cover southern and eastern Russia. Mount Elbrus, in the Western Caucasus range, is the highest point. It is a dormant volcano.

Lake Baikal in southern Siberia is the world's deepest lake. It holds approximately 20 percent of the world's fresh surface water. The Volga River runs through central Russia. It is the longest river in Europe. Many people think of it as the country's national river.

Russia contains many different climates, from its arctic north to **arid** south. Winters are usually extremely cold. Summers are hot or mild, depending on the area. Moscow, in the western part of the country, has a temperature range of 12 to 76 degrees Fahrenheit (−11 to 24 degrees Celsius). In other locations, the average annual temperature is below freezing, or 32°F (0°C).

The southern lakes have a much milder climate than regions to the north. Many Russians go on vacations to resort towns there during the summer.

Land of Extremes

Russia is often described as a land of extremes. The Kamchatka Peninsula is one example. It is sometimes called a land of fire and ice. Between the Bering Sea and the Sea of Okhotsk, the peninsula juts out into the water. Hot springs and active volcanoes give way to snowy mountains and glaciers.

In 2017, an estimated 15 percent of city-dwelling Russians breathed unhealthy air.

Factories and mines have created many environmental problems. Air pollution is a problem in Russia's big cities. It also affects smaller factory towns. Nuclear waste from power plants is another concern. **Radioactive contamination** is found in the soil in some areas. Today, people are working to clean up Russia's environment.

Many of Russia's unique animals are **endangered** or threatened. Fewer than 100 Amur leopards are left in southeastern Russia. Siberian tigers live in the same area. There are fewer than 500 left.

A variety of plants grow in Russia. Lichens are a combination of algae and fungi. They are found in the northernmost regions.

Norilsk, Russia

The mining city of Norilsk is in the Arctic Circle. It is the world's northernmost large city and has a population of more than 100,000. People work in palladium mines and factories. This rare metal is necessary for making cell phones. Norilsk is Russia's most polluted city and one of the most polluted cities in the world. Most of the area's plants and animals have died off.

CHAPTER 2

BUSINESS AND GOVERNMENT IN RUSSIA

Russia's roots as a country date back to an eastern **Slavic** state. It was formed in the 9th century. Later, rulers called tsars controlled the land. In the 17th and 18th centuries, tsars greatly expanded the Russian Empire. Russia's economy and government have gone through many changes since then.

Christianity was introduced to Russia in the 9th century.

In 1917, revolutionaries overthrew Tsar Nicholas II. Russia became a **communist** state known as the Union of Soviet Socialist Republics. It was more often called the U.S.S.R. or Soviet Union. The state owned all the property and businesses.

People grew unhappy with communism. They wanted more freedom. The U.S.S.R. collapsed in 1991. Russia and 14 other countries were created. Today, the economy is no longer completely controlled by the state. Some companies are owned privately. The government still owns certain major businesses, like oil and natural gas companies.

Tsar Nicholas II was seen as weak and inept.

Russian Rubles

The ruble is Russia's standard currency. It can take the form of both paper money and coins. A ruble is divided into 100 kopecks. In 2019, one U.S. dollar equaled approximately 66.3 Russian rubles.

Around 67 percent of workers are in the service industry. This includes government jobs, finance, and transportation. Almost 27 percent work in heavy industry, including mining and energy production. Agricultural jobs account for around 6 percent of the workforce.

Beekeeping has a long tradition in Russia, and is now a growing part of the agriculture industry.

Russia produces about 12 percent of the world's oil.

Energy is the most important part of Russia's economy. Oil and natural gas make up almost 59 percent of Russia's **exports**.

Russia also **imports** items from different countries. Medications and cars make up many of these products. The nation also brings in planes, helicopters, and spacecraft. These are used by the country's army.

Only 13 percent of Russia's land is used for agriculture. One of the most important crops is wheat. Russia is the top exporter of wheat in the world. Sunflowers are the second most profitable crop. More than 20 percent of the world's sunflower oil is produced there. Farmers also grow oats, potatoes, and barley.

2018 TRADING PARTNERS

Russia has many important trading partners. Many are nearby in Asia or Europe. Trading partners are the countries where Russia sends its exports or where its imports come from. Here is a graph showing Russia's top import and export trading partners as of 2018.

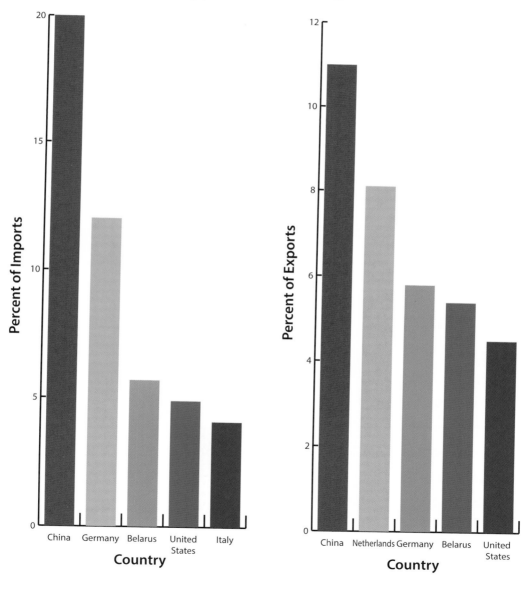

Today, Russia is a semi-presidential **federation**. It is ruled by a president and a prime minister. The legislative branch is called the Federal Assembly. This is made up of the Federation Council (upper house) and the State Duma (lower house).

The Russian White House is the office of the Russian prime minister and much of the Russian government.

Russian Flag

Russia's national flag was officially adopted in 1991. It had first been used on ships in 1699. The flag features three horizontal stripes of the same length and width. The top stripe is white, the middle one is blue, and the bottom stripe is red.

ACTIVITY

Russia's national anthem is *"Gosudarstvennyy Gimn Rossiyskoy Federatsii"* ("National Anthem of the Russian Federation"). The lyrics have been changed several times since the music was written in the late 1930s. This is not very common for national anthems. The lyrics often reflect changes in the country's values and priorities after major events.

Look online to research some of the changes. Make a timeline with three to five important dates. What did you learn about Russia's history through the anthem's history?

The most recent change to the national anthem was in 2000.

Russian president Vladimir Putin is the longest-serving leader of Russia since Joseph Stalin.

Power in Russia starts with the president. He chooses a prime minister and cabinet members. Citizens elect their leader by popular vote to a 6-year term. There have been many accusations of corruption surrounding recent presidential elections.

Vladimir Putin served as president of Russia from 2000 to 2008. He was only allowed two terms in a row. He stepped down and became prime minister. Dmitry Medvedev was the next president. Then, Putin was reelected twice more, starting in 2012. At this point, terms were extended from 4 to 6 years.

The nation's next election is in 2024. At the beginning of 2020, Putin signaled that he would not give up power in 2024. After Putin suggested changing the Constitution to allow this, the prime minister and his government resigned.

Many things have improved since the hardships of the Soviet era. Work and politics are only two parts of Russian life.

Russia and Ukraine

The country of Ukraine borders Russia to the west. It was part of the Soviet Union until 1991. Before that, it was controlled by the Russian Empire. Today, it is an independent country, but it still has a complicated relationship with Russia. Crimea is a disputed area between the two countries. Russia took control of it again in 2014.

CHAPTER 3

MEET THE PEOPLE

Around 144.5 million people live in Russia, making it the ninth most populous country in the world. Around 74 percent live in **urban** areas, mostly in the western part of the country. Many small villages are disappearing today as people move to cities.

Moscow is the largest city in Russia and the second largest in Europe. The population is over 12 million.

The Bashkirs are one of many ethnic groups in Russia.

St. Petersburg's population is approximately 5.4 million. Tsar Peter the Great founded the city in 1703. It was the capital for around 200 years and is still considered the cultural capital. Many important buildings are found there.

Novosibirsk is the main city in the Asian portion of Russia. Its population is around 1.5 million. This is much smaller than the cities in the west.

Whether in a city or rural village, family is very important to Russians. Multiple generations often live together in the same home.

Several different cultural groups live in Russia. Around 78 percent are native Russians. The Tatars, Bashkirs, and Chuvash ethnic groups make up around 6 percent. Around 1 percent of the population is originally from Ukraine.

The Russian people have many long-standing traditions, including jumping over bonfires at midsummer festivals.

The country's official language is Russian. This is a Slavic language that uses the Cyrillic alphabet. Letters are based on the Greek alphabet. In the English alphabet, letters are based on the Roman alphabet. Russian is used by the government and in schools. However, there are 35 other official languages that are used in different regions. Around 4.2 million Russians speak Tatar. Chechen and Bashkir have more than 1 million speakers each.

А Б В Г Д Е
Ё Ж З И Й К
Л М Н О П Р
С Т У Ф Х Ц
Ч Ш Щ Ъ Ы
Ь Э Ю Я

The Cyrillic alphabet has 33 letters.

Baba Yaga

There are many different folktales in Russian culture. One popular figure is Baba Yaga. This character sometimes appears as an evil witch. In other cases, she is described as a wise old woman. Her house sits on top of chicken legs. There is usually a lesson or moral in stories about Baba Yaga.

In Russia, children start school at age 6 or 7. They spend their first year learning how to read and write. Students are required to stay in school until they are 15 or 16 years old. They often stay with the same classmates from year to year.

Some students decide to keep studying. Vocational training to learn a specific job is one option. Others take more classes to prepare to go to university.

In the U.S.S.R., every student in the country wore the same uniform. Now, most students still wear uniforms, but they can vary from school to school.

ACTIVITY

Matryoshka dolls are sets of wooden dolls that are usually dressed in traditional Russian clothing. Each doll in the set is smaller than the next. The dolls can be opened and are stacked from smallest to biggest. When they are stacked like this, it looks like there is only one. Some have themes. They look like historical leaders or characters from fairy tales.

MATERIALS:

- Paper cups
- Glue stick
- Construction paper
- Scrapbook or patterned paper
- Pens

INSTRUCTIONS:

1. Cut circles from the construction paper for faces and decorate with the pens.

2. Cut shawls, bodies, and tummy panels from the scrapbook paper.

3. Glue these onto the cups to make a doll on each cup.

4. Stack the cups to make your own set of *matryoshka* dolls.

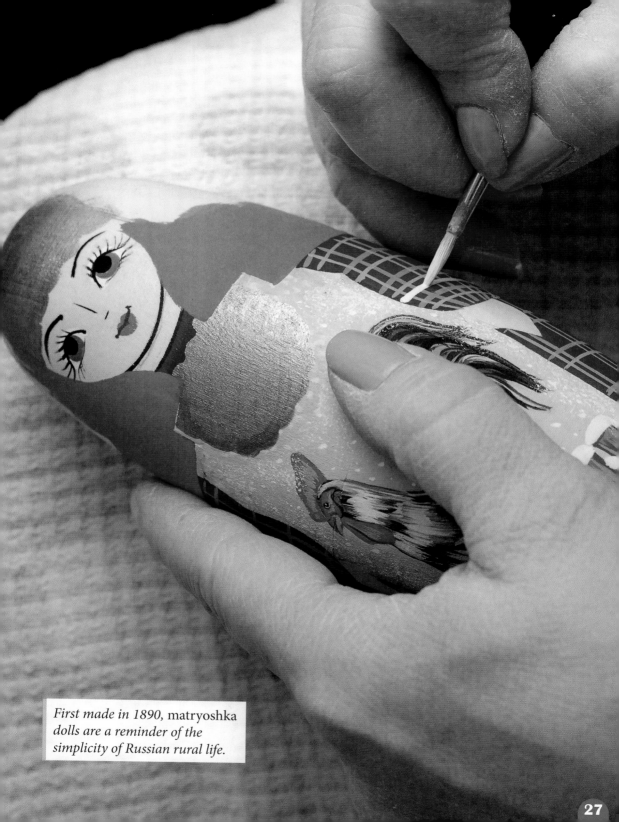

First made in 1890, matryoshka dolls are a reminder of the simplicity of Russian rural life.

Ballet has been practiced seriously in Russia since the 1700s, and Russian ballet is a distinct style.

The U.S.S.R. operated centers where children could do activities for free. Private clubs were not allowed. Today, the government still runs centers with free athletics or art lessons. Popular sports are soccer, hockey, and swimming. Some parents send their children to private clubs after school. Kids can take ice-skating or dance lessons. Special sports schools offer education along with intense training. Student athletes are trained for the Olympics.

CHAPTER 4

CELEBRATIONS

Food, music, and dancing are all important parts of Russian holidays. Religious and national holidays give people a chance to celebrate with family and friends.

Russia's biggest holidays take place during the winter. On New Year's Eve, children wait for Father Frost and his daughter the Snow Maiden to deliver presents. New Year's Day is a huge celebration. Families host big meals, sing carols, give gifts, and watch fireworks.

Russian folk dances originated in the 10th century. The costumes are often very elaborate.

Russian Orthodox Christmas is an important religious holiday. This falls on January 7 instead of December 25, which is the common date in other parts of the world. The Russian Orthodox Church uses the **Julian calendar** to plan its holidays. Most other Christian groups follow the **Gregorian calendar** instead.

Easter is another religious holiday that many Russians celebrate. It falls in the spring, although the exact date varies. It is also on the Julian calendar. People celebrate with a special dish called *pashka*. This dessert is similar to cheesecake.

HOLIDAYS AND CELEBRATIONS

January 1 – **New Year's Day**

January 7 – **Russian Orthodox Christmas**

February 23 – **Defender of the Fatherland Day**

February or March (8 weeks before Easter) – **Maslenitsa**

March 8 – **International Women's Day**

April 12 – **Cosmonaut's Da**y

April or May (date changes) – **Orthodox Easter**

May 1 – **Spring and Labor Day**

May 9 – **Victory Day**

June 12 – **Russia Day**

September 1 – **Knowledge Day**

November 4 – **National Unity Day**

Pashka *is often brought to church to be blessed before Easter.*

ACTIVITY

When the tsars ruled Russia, members of the royal family often exchanged Fabergé eggs at Easter. These jeweled creations are made of precious metals and gemstones. During modern Easter celebrations, many children decorate eggs.

MATERIALS:

- Pencil
- Construction paper (multiple colors)
- Scissors
- Crayons or markers
- Glue
- Glitter
- Sequins

INSTRUCTIONS:

1. Use a pencil to trace a large, oval-shaped outline of an egg on a sheet of construction paper.

2. Cut out your egg using scissors. Lay the cutout on a clean, flat surface.

3. Decide how you want to decorate the egg. Real Fabergé eggs feature detailed designs. They sparkle with precious metals and jewels. Use crayons or markers to sketch diamonds and other gems on your paper egg. Glue glitter and shiny sequins to your egg in creative designs.

4. Allow the glue to dry completely.

5. Make several Fabergé eggs. Then give them to friends and family members as special springtime gifts.

Russian Easter eggs can also be decorated or wrapped with colorful designs.

Other Russian holidays honor the country's history. Victory Day is May 9. It celebrates Russia's triumphs during World War II (1939–1945). Military parades are held in different cities. In Moscow, soldiers march through Red Square. This is just outside the Kremlin, where Russia's government is based.

On June 12, Russians observe Russia Day. This holiday marks the country's declaration of independence from Soviet control in 1990. Many cities celebrate with festivals and fireworks.

A group of soldiers called the Kremlin Regiment takes part in parades.

Maslenitsa is a festival that is held 8 weeks before Russian Orthodox Easter. Even though it takes place in February or March, it symbolizes the end of winter and the start of spring. Festivities run for a full week. It is also known as "Pancake Week." Here is a look at each day's activities.

Monday: A Maslenitsa doll made of straw is brought into town on a sleigh. People start celebrating by eating blini, or pancakes, around 5:00 p.m.

Tuesday: Games Day includes puppet shows and sleigh rides.

Wednesday: Gourmand, or Sweet Day, centers on many different kinds of blini.

Thursday: Revelry Day has more games. Ice-skating is a popular activity.

Friday: Traditionally, mothers-in-law were celebrated. During modern festivals, all mothers are honored.

Saturday: Families celebrate with more games and activities. This is a big day since people don't have to go to work.

Sunday: The Maslenitsa doll is burned on a bonfire. This represents the end of winter and the beginning of spring.

Monday: Lent begins.

Religion is a very important part of Russian life. Around 70 percent of Russians are members of the Russian Orthodox Church. This is an offshoot of Catholicism that has its own rites and rituals. Roughly 10 percent of Russia's citizens are Muslim. A small percentage of residents practice the Jewish faith.

The Church of the Savior on Spilled Blood is a Russian Orthodox cathedral. It is known for its iconic onion domes.

Tengrism is a growing religion. It used to be practiced all over Siberia during the time of Genghis Khan. Now, it is gaining in popularity again, especially with people who live near the borders of Mongolia and China. They want to feel a connection to their Central Asian heritage.

CHAPTER 5

WHAT'S FOR DINNER?

Food plays a big part in Russian holidays. Thin pancakes called blini are served on Maslenitsa and for other celebrations. They are often rolled with sweet fillings inside, like jam or chocolate. Sometimes, they are prepared as a savory dish with meat and vegetables.

Caviar, or raw fish eggs, are often served with buckwheat blini.

Everyday meals in Russia are usually hearty. Vegetables like potatoes, beets, and cabbage are commonly used. Meat makes up an important part of the diet. Beef, chicken, pork, and fish can all be found in Russian dishes. Sour cream and butter are often added. Many people eat bread with their meals. They eat it with cheese or jam. After dinner, tea with sugar is served.

Jam is not only eaten on bread, but also put into tea and even eaten by itself.

Soup

Many meals in Russia include soup. Soup can be served cold in the summer or hot in the winter. Some people even put ice in soup to keep it cold. The most common hot soup is borscht. It is made out of beets and flavored with dill and sour cream.

One of the biggest influences on Russian food has been the weather. Long, cold winters meant that fresh food had to be prepared so it could last for several months. Pickling vegetables is one technique that uses vinegar or salt. Today, many people still eat pickled vegetables along with their meals. Drying, smoking, and salting meat and fish are other ways to preserve food. Kefir is a drink that is similar to yogurt. It is made through fermentation, which makes it last longer without going bad.

Kefir is often flavored with fruit or herbs.

Cabbage, peppers, carrots, and beets are just some of the foods pickled in Russia.

Different herbs and spices are used in Russian dishes. Dill was often used to help pickle foods. Now, it is added toward the end of cooking to give meals more flavor. Garlic stayed fresh during long winters. It is found in many soup, stew, and meat recipes. Other common flavors are parsley and tarragon.

Appetizers

Appetizers are an important part of meals in Russia. They are often served buffet-style for holidays. These dishes might be something simple like stuffed eggs or pickled vegetables. Others are fancier like caviar. *Kholodets* is a type of meat jelly that takes more than 7 hours to prepare. It is a popular dish to eat on New Year's Eve.

Stuffed dishes are another popular way of cooking. Pierogi, or *vareniki*, are dumplings filled with meat, cheese, or potatoes. Pelmeni are smaller dumplings. They are usually stuffed with meat. At first, they were popular in the Ural Mountains. Now, people all over Russia enjoy them.

Pierogi are made all over Eastern Europe.

RECIPE

Blini is a popular dish to have around holidays. People love eating blini with friends and family to celebrate. This recipe requires using a stove. Ask an adult to help you.

INGREDIENTS:

- 1 cup (128 grams) of flour
- ½ teaspoon (3 g) of salt
- ½ tsp (2.4 g) of baking powder
- 1 cup of milk minus 2 tablespoons (about 210 milliliters of milk total)
- 1 large egg
- 1 tbsp (15 ml) of melted butter

Blini can also be served with caviar.

INSTRUCTIONS:

1. Combine the flour, salt, and baking powder in a bowl.
2. In a separate bowl, use a whisk to stir the milk, egg, and butter together.
3. Pour the liquid mixture into the flour mixture and stir until combined.
4. Heat 1 tablespoon (15 ml) of butter in a skillet over medium-low heat.
5. Drop 1 tablespoon (15 ml) of batter into the heated skillet. Cook until bubbles form, about 1.5 to 2 minutes.
6. Flip the blini and cook until it's brown, about 1 minute.
7. Place on plate lined with paper towel.
8. Repeat with remaining batter.
9. Serve blini with your favorite jam and sour cream.

French chefs cooked for wealthy Russian families in the 19th century. One chef created beef stroganoff. It is flavored with French mustard but also with sour cream, in a more Russian style.

Beef stroganoff is often served with egg noodles. It can also be served with rice.

In the U.S.S.R., workers ate in canteens, or cafeterias. Meals were prepared with simple techniques and ingredients. Russians started to cook at home the same way.

From food to festivals, history to wildlife, Russia is exciting to explore. It would take years to see all the sights in this huge nation!

The round pastries called baranki *are not only treats eaten with tea, but also traditional symbols of prosperity.*

GLOSSARY

arid *(EH-ruhd)* a climate with little or no rain, or that cannot support much plant life

communist *(KOM-yuh-nist)* having to do with a type of government with an economy that is based on public or state control of property and business

endangered *(in-DAYN-juhrd)* at risk of dying out completely

exports *(EK-sports)* acts of selling something to another country or products sold in this way

federation *(fed-ur-AY-shun)* a collection of territories and regions that are represented by a central government or joined together by some type of agreement

Gregorian calendar *(gri-GOR-ee-uhn KAL-en-dur)* a calendar system used by much of the international world

imports *(IM-ports)* brings something from another country to sell

Julian calendar *(JOO-lee-uhn KAL-en-dur)* a calendar system used by certain countries and religions

radioactive contamination *(ray-dee-oh-AK-tiv kon-ta-mih-NAY-shun)* when potentially harmful radioactive waste is deposited where it is not desired

Slavic *(SLAH-vik)* having to do with a family of languages that includes Russian, Polish, and others or with a speaker of those languages

tundra *(TUHN-druh)* a flat northern area with no trees where the ground is always frozen

urban *(UR-bin)* having to do with cities

FOR MORE INFORMATION

BOOKS

Baby Professor. *Russia for Kids: People, Places and Cultures.* Newark, DE: Speedy Publishing LLC, 2015.

Burton, Jesse. *Russia.* New York, NY: Simon Spotlight, 2018.

Kalz, Jill. *My First Russian Phrases.* North Mankato, MN: Picture Window Books, 2012.

WEBSITES

Central Intelligence Agency—The World Factbook: Russia
https://www.cia.gov/library/publications/the-world-factbook/geos/rs.html
Check out this site for information about Russia's economy, geography, population, and government.

Kids World Travel Guide—Russia Facts for Kids
https://www.kids-world-travel-guide.com/russia-facts.html
You'll find information about Russian history and more at this helpful site.

National Geographic Kids—Russia
https://kids.nationalgeographic.com/Places/Find/Russia
Scan this site for an overview of Russia, from geographic information to cultural highlights.

INDEX

ABOUT THE AUTHOR

Meghan Gottschall is a writer and former university lecturer in French. She loves to travel to new places, but has to admit it's been a while. Meghan currently lives in the Midwest with her husband and two young sons.